Dale the snail was  town shared with critters.

As he grew into his shell, he realized he was different than the other snails.

While all snails are slimy, Dale was REALLY slimy. So slimy in fact, that some of the other snails would tease him about it.

But that was just how Dale was born and he could not change it. Even though he was a little different, he was truly just like all the other snails.

As other snails continued to tease him, he did not want to be in public anymore and he became very sad.

Dale's good friend Doug would come over to visit and would always encourage Dale to not worry about what others thought of him.

While it was nice having Doug around, Dale still felt down and isolated from the outside world.

One day when Doug came over to check on Dale, he had an idea.

Doug thought that Dale could use his slime to his benefit, rather than be ashamed of it.

The routes that all the snails and slugs take on the sidewalk were always slow. This was because their slime trails would dry up too quickly to be used by others.

Doug felt that Dale's extra slime could create a snail trail across the sidewalk for others to use.

These trails could work as a gliding path that could speed up everyone's daily commutes.

Dale was hesitant about the idea because he would be helping the snails that would make fun of him.

Why should he help them?

Dale realized that it shouldn't matter what a few snails say about him. He would be helping a lot of others that accept him for who he is.

He also realized that he could be brave and not let any bullies change who he is meant to be!

While it would be scary to go out into the world, Dale wanted to be courageous and face his fears.

With full determination and belief in himself, he started planning the snail trail express.

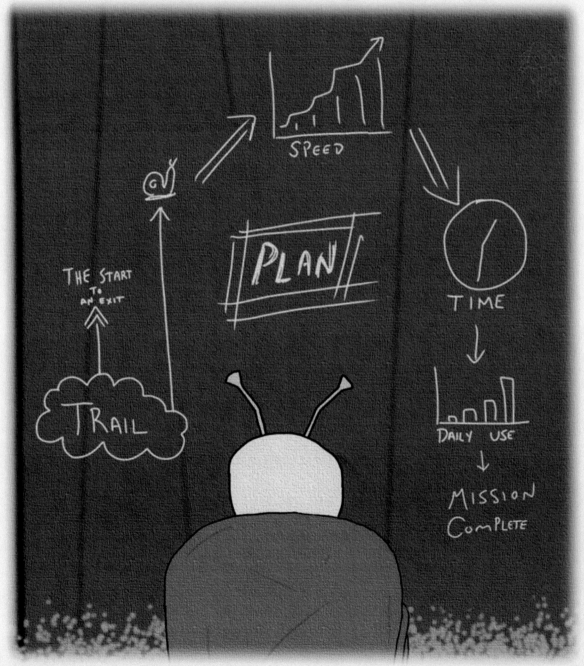

Dale worked day and night, leaning on motivation from Doug to help him stay focused and determined.

With a plan in place, he would begin his trail services to his community the next morning.

Early the following day, Dale took a look at himself before venturing out and he realized how nervous he truly was.

But he remained determined!

Once at the sidewalk, Dale got to work. He started paving the slimy trail before anyone else was awake.

As everyone started their daily commute, they noticed Dale's trail system across the sidewalk.

They were amazed! This trail saved them an immense amount of time, as they could now quickly move across the sidewalk with ease!

Dale stayed nearby to ensure everything went smoothly, but the snails that had teased him started to approach.

Terrified, Dale tucked into his shell.
His worst fear was becoming a
reality in front of his very eyes!

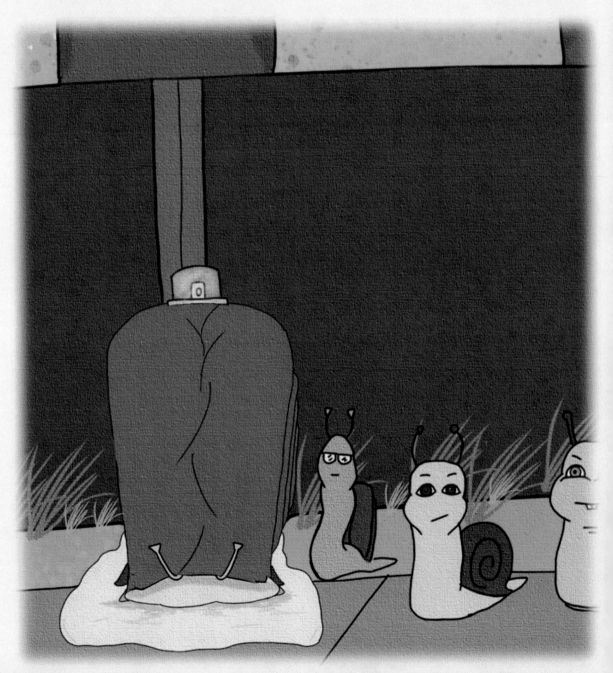

With a gentle tap on his shell, they asked if they could talk. It was time to face his bullies...

To his relief, they wanted to thank him for all of his hard work and to apologize for how they had treated him in the past.

They were so thankful, they brought Dale some lunch. A berry – his favorite!

Dale was elated! He was so proud to see the appreciation of his hard work and tenacity.

He was asked if he could continue to provide the snail trail because it was so helpful.

Dale had the courage to face his fears, which positively changed his life and those around him.

He realized that we should not be so hard on ourselves, be proud of who we are, and embrace our differences!

Thank you for reading our book! We are a veteran family that wants to share our passion for art and education. We also want to encourage kids to love themselves for who they are and to not be discouraged by others.

Again, we THANK YOU!

Shane flying in an MH-60 helicopter near Kabul, Afghanistan